TRIPLE H

by **Michael Sandler**

Consultant: Eric Cohen
Wrestling Expert
prowrestling.about.com

BEARPORT PUBLISHING

New York, New York

Credits

Cover and Title Page, © Getty Images; TOC, © Bob Levey/WireImage/Getty Images; 4, © Matt Roberts/ZUMA Press/Newscom; 5T, © Matt Roberts/Zuma Press/Newscom; 5B, © Rex/Rex USA/ BEImages; 6, © Matt Roberts/ZUMA Press/Newscom; 7, © John Barrett/Globe Photos/ZUMA Press; 9, © Exactostock/SuperStock; 10, © Kevin Winter/Getty Images; 11, © Stephen Harman/ Newspix/News Ltd.; 12, © B. Bennett/Getty Images; 13, © AP Photo/Jon Chase; 14, © John Rodeo; 15, © Duomo/Corbis; 15, © Jim Bourg/Reuters/Landov; 16L, © Matt Roberts/ZUMA Press/ Newscom; 16R, © Craig Lassig/AFP/Getty Images; 17, © John Barrett/Globe Photos/ZUMA Press; 19, © George Pimentel/WireImage/Getty Images; 20, © AP Photo/StarPix/Dave Allocca; 21, © David Seto; 22T, © George Pimentel/WireImage/Getty Images; 22B, © Bob Levey/WireImage/ Getty Images.

Publisher: Kenn Goin
Senior Editor: Lisa Wiseman
Creative Director: Spencer Brinker
Photo Researcher: We Research Pictures, LLC
Design: Debrah Kaiser

Library of Congress Cataloging-in-Publication Data

Sandler, Michael, 1965–
  Triple H / by Michael Sandler ; consultant, Eric Cohen.
    p. cm. — (Wrestling's tough guys)
  Includes bibliographical references and index.
  ISBN 978-1-61772-575-3 (library binding) — ISBN 1-61772-575-7 (library binding)
  1. Triple H., 1969—Juvenile literature. 2. Wrestlers—United States—Biography—Juvenile literature. I. Cohen, Eric. II. Title.
  GV1196.T75S26 2013
  796.812092—dc23
  [B]
                                    2012010034

For more information, write to Bearport Publishing Company, Inc., 45 West 21st Street, Suite 3B, New York, New York 10010. Printed in the United States of America.

10 9 8 7 6 5 4 3 2 1

Contents

Showdown with the Punk

On September 18, 2011, Triple H walked toward the ring and his opponent, CM Punk. The two **rivals** glared at each other. This match was going to be ugly!

Before he got into the ring, Triple H turned to salute the crowd. That's when CM Punk snuck up from behind and slammed Triple H's head with a **forearm** smash. The match hadn't even begun, but already the two men were battling.

Triple H

Triple H wasn't just a wrestler. He was also one of the WWE's top **executives**. More than just a win was at stake for him. If he lost to CM Punk, Triple H had promised to give up his job.

When the bell rang to signal the start of the match, the two wrestlers were outside the ring, hurling each other across the announcers' tables. The referee was helpless in this **no disqualification match**. The rules meant nothing!

CM Punk in action with Randy Orton

CM Punk

Still the Boss

As the battle raged on, the action occurred both inside and outside the ring. At one point, CM Punk kicked Triple H into a set of metal steps. Then he climbed to the top rope of the ring and leaped at Triple H, hoping to deliver a match-ending blow.

CM Punk gets ready to jump from the top rope during another match.

Triple H was ready, however. As CM Punk jumped from the rope, Triple H kicked him hard. Then he smashed CM Punk to the mat with his **signature move**—the Pedigree.

CM Punk squirmed away, however, avoiding the **pin**. A few minutes later, Triple H delivered a match-ending Pedigree. He had defeated CM Punk, and by winning, he got to keep his job.

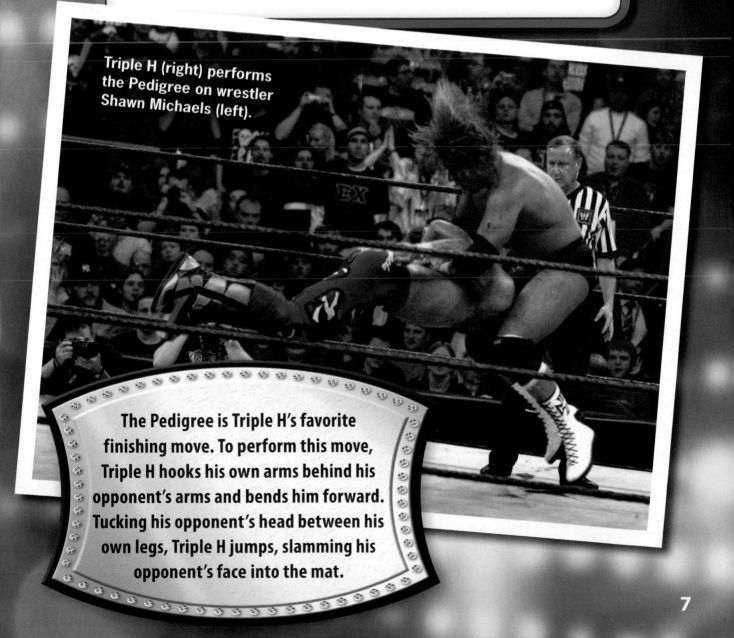

Triple H (right) performs the Pedigree on wrestler Shawn Michaels (left).

The Pedigree is Triple H's favorite finishing move. To perform this move, Triple H hooks his own arms behind his opponent's arms and bends him forward. Tucking his opponent's head between his own legs, Triple H jumps, slamming his opponent's face into the mat.

A Roadside Sign

While growing up in New Hampshire, Paul Michael Levesque had no idea he would one day become Triple H. In fact, it took a lucky car ride to start him on the path to wrestling stardom. One afternoon, the skinny 14-year-old was riding with a friend. They saw a sign advertising a new local gym called Muscles in Motion. The gym offered free passes, good for a week of training.

Paul Michael Levesque was born on July 27, 1969, and grew up in Nashua, New Hampshire.

Let's try it, they thought. Once inside the gym, Paul was immediately blown away. He heard barbells clinking. He saw powerful **bodybuilders** lifting huge weights. He thought it was the coolest place he'd ever been. He knew right away he wanted to join.

Bodybuilders often spend years lifting heavier and heavier weights to develop their bodies.

As a teen, Paul delivered newspapers. He used the money he earned to pay for his gym membership.

Building the Body

Soon after joining the gym, Paul was heading there every single day. He loved working out. He especially loved that everyone at the gym was serious about making their bodies strong.

Although he rarely had time to see his friends, Paul didn't mind. Bodybuilding was his passion. He pushed himself harder and harder, trying to keep up with the older, stronger bodybuilders who also worked out at the gym.

Triple H shows off his strong arms in 2001.

By his late teens, Paul was competing in bodybuilding contests—and winning them! Still, Paul had another goal in mind. He wanted to use his new strength to become a pro wrestler.

Triple H, shown here in 2009, has spent countless hours in the gym getting into top shape.

At 17 years old, Paul was six feet four inches (1.93 m) tall and packed 210 pounds (95 kg) of muscle.

Learning to Wrestle

   As a kid, Paul had always loved pro wrestling. He watched it on TV and bought wrestling magazines. Now, with his new stronger body, Paul decided to see if he could become a pro wrestler himself. His first step was enrolling at Walter "Killer" Kowalski's School of Professional Wrestling in the early 1990s.

Paul's childhood wrestling hero was Ric Flair (shown here).

The wrestling school was about an hour away from Paul's New Hampshire home. Paul drove there on weekends to learn everything he could. Walter was a tough coach. Many students quit. They couldn't keep up with his hard workouts. Paul, however, loved them. His hard work quickly earned him Walter's **confidence**.

Walter "Killer" Kowalski (left) with his nephew in 1989

Just four months after Paul began training at Walter's school, he made his pro wrestling start. It wasn't a big event in a huge arena—Paul earned just $25— but it was a start.

The Big Time

Soon, Paul began traveling around New England wrestling in small gyms. At this time, he wasn't using the name Triple H yet. He was going by the **ring name** Terra Ryzing. He chose it because it sounded dangerous—like the word *terrorizing*. Paul was having fun wrestling, but he wanted more. He wanted to face superstars such as Ric Flair, not just local wrestlers.

Paul (left) as Terra Ryzing in the ring before a match in 1993

After about a year, Paul made his move. In 1994, he joined the **WCW**, a wrestling group with big-name wrestlers that televised its matches. A year later, he switched to the WWE. By doing so, Paul had joined the most **elite** wrestling organization in the world. He soon started going by the new name Triple H.

Triple H in action a few years after joining the WWE

Triple H stands for the initials of Paul's ring name: Hunter Hearst Helmsley. He's also frequently called by another nickname—The Game.

The Toughest Champion

As a member of the WWE, Triple H was taking on the world's greatest wrestlers and winning titles, too. In 1996, he beat "Wildman" Marc Mero to take the **Intercontinental Championship**. Then in 1999, he won the **WWE Championship** by defeating Mankind.

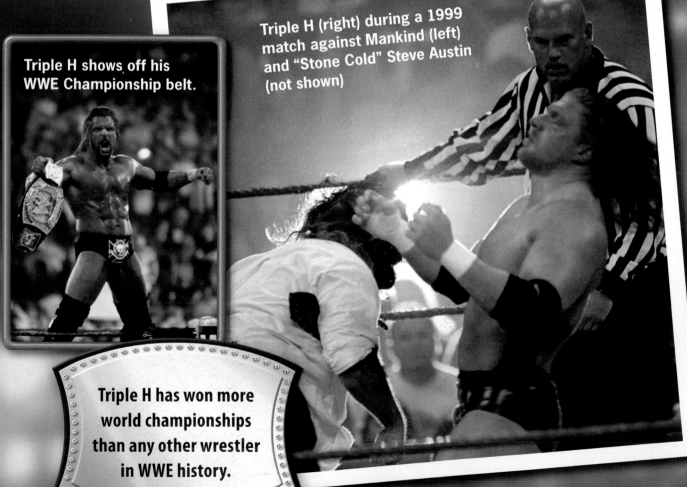

Triple H shows off his WWE Championship belt.

Triple H (right) during a 1999 match against Mankind (left) and "Stone Cold" Steve Austin (not shown)

Triple H has won more world championships than any other wrestler in WWE history.

Even when he lost, Triple H showed unmatchable toughness. In a 2001 **tag-team** match with "Stone Cold" Steve Austin against Chris Jericho and Chris Benoit, Triple H ripped the **quadriceps** muscle in his left leg. Pain tore through his body. Most wrestlers would have quit instantly. Triple H, however, kept wrestling until the match was over.

Triple H (right) about to attack Chris Jericho (left) during a match in 2000

Better Than Ever

After the match, Triple H discovered just how serious his muscle injury was. He needed to stop wrestling for about seven months to **rehabilitate** his injured leg. The rehab was slow and painful, but Triple H never thought about quitting. "Giving one hundred percent... was the only thing I considered," he said.

In 2002, Triple H was healthy enough to return to wrestling. His first match was the 2002 **Royal Rumble**. "The Game is back," shouted the announcer. It turned out he was better than ever. Triple H tore though one wrestler after another, for the win and the prize— the right to fight for the WWE Championship at WrestleMania X8!

Just two months after the Royal Rumble, Triple H won his fifth WWE Championship at WrestleMania X8. To do so, he beat Chris Jericho, the wrestler whom he'd injured himself against the year before.

Triple H (right) kicks Chris Jericho (left) during WrestleMania X8.

The Love of Wrestling

Triple H is known as one of the greatest wrestlers in WWE history. He's more than just an athlete; he's also a WWE executive who helps run the organization. He has plenty to keep him busy besides wrestling, but nothing can keep him outside the ring.

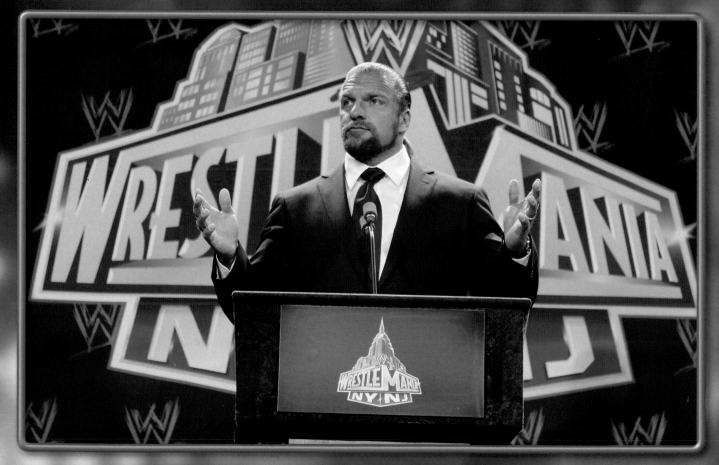

Triple H spends part of his time helping run the WWE. Here he is at a news conference in 2012.

After two decades in the sport, Triple H loves wrestling just as much as when he first started. It's not about fame, or even money. If he won $500 million in the lottery, he has said, he still wouldn't quit wrestling. "I'd still do this. I just love it," he said.

Triple H shakes hands with his fans.

Triple H is a five-time World Heavyweight Champion and an eight-time WWE Champion. He is also the winner of the 2002 Royal Rumble.

The Triple H File

Stats:

Born:	July 27, 1969, Nashua, New Hampshire
Height:	6' 4" (1.93 m)
Weight:	255 pounds (116 kg)
Greatest Moves:	Pedigree, Facebreaker Knee Smash, Spinning Spinebuster

Fun Facts:

- As a child, Paul played baseball and basketball, but he lost interest in team sports by junior high. Wrestling was the only sport that he wanted to participate in.

- As a teen bodybuilder, Paul won the Teenage Mr. New Hampshire competition in 1988.

- Triple H is married to Stephanie McMahon, a former wrestler and daughter of the head of the WWE, Vince McMahon.

Triple H (left) battles Randy Orton (right) in 2009.